Original title:
Tales Told by Tall Trees

Copyright © 2025 Creative Arts Management OÜ
All rights reserved.

Author: Zachary Prescott
ISBN HARDBACK: 978-1-80567-308-8
ISBN PAPERBACK: 978-1-80567-607-2

The Grove's Gentle Murmurs

In the grove where laughter sways,
Branches dance in sunny rays.
Squirrels wear their acorn crowns,
Whispering secrets, spinning gowns.

An owl hoots with a silly grin,
While chipmunks race, it's a mad spin.
Blades of grass join in the cheer,
As the breeze brings giggles near.

Among the bark, a raccoon peers,
Telling jokes that spark wild cheers.
Each leaf sways like a dancer's twirl,
Crafting mischief in a whirl.

A frog croaks out a silly tune,
While bees buzz round like a cartoon.
Nature's humor fills the air,
In the grove, with joy to share.

Age of Arbor

In the age where trees can talk,
They giggle softly as they walk.
A lumberjack with a comical hat,
Trips on roots, oh what of that!

The trees recall when they were small,
With dreams of reaching way up tall.
Now they share their wit and age,
Scripting laughs upon their page.

Woodpeckers drum like a band in play,
Calling for squirrels to join the fray.
Acorns drop with a ponderous thud,
They bounce like laughter's joyful flood.

Under the shade where shadows lounge,
A cat naps, making no sound.
But trees catch whispers that transpire,
And giggle softly, never tire.

Secrets in the Shadows

In the shadows where stories creep,
Squirrels giggle, never sleep.
Behind the trunks, the whispers flow,
Carried by winds that twist and blow.

The fabled owl cracks a light joke,
As fireflies twinkle, never broke.
Mice in glasses share their schemes,
Plotting mischief in moonlit dreams.

The pine trees whisper, tales they cling,
Of silly things that tramps might bring.
Under the cover of leaf and vine,
Nature's humor, perfectly fine.

A raccoon spins around with glee,
Stealing snacks and climbing trees.
Secrets hidden in the shade,
In the shadows, laughter's made.

Mythos of the Green Giants

In a park where squirrels leap,
A giant lost a shoe, not cheap.
With acorns flying through the air,
The trees just laughed without a care.

The birds all chirped a silly tune,
While branches danced beneath the moon.
One tree claimed it was quite tall,
But the other teased, "You're just a wall!"

Leaves giggled in the sunny glow,
As beams of light began to flow.
A raccoon whispered, "Is that a vine?"
The tree replied, "No, it's just a line!"

So here we stand, both bark and cheer,
With every whisper, loud and clear.
Among the giants, laughter reigns,
In their shade, the fun remains.

Chronicles of the Rooted Guardians

Underneath the big, wise oak,
A bunny told a funny joke.
About a worm that danced all night,
With roots that twirled in sheer delight.

The maple blushed, turned a bright red,
Said, "You cracked me up, now I'll spread!"
With branches swaying left and right,
They laughed till dusk, with all their might.

A crow flew in, wings all aflutter,
Singing songs of nutty butter.
The trees swayed with a chuckle loud,
Claiming their bark was just too proud.

Each ring holds a secret grin,
Of all the stories tucked within.
Join the fun where laughter grows,
In every leaf, a giggle flows.

The Silence of Timbered Giants

Silent trees with leafy crowns,
Whisper jokes in leafy gowns.
One tree said, "I'm growing wide,"
The other replied, "Well, I'm the pride!"

In the stillness, silly hugs,
From little bugs and wiggly rugs.
A pine declared, with utmost glee,
"I've got the best cones, can't you see?"

A gust of wind, a playful tease,
Leaves did waltz, oh what a breeze!
Knots giggled, as shadows played,
In the quiet, joys displayed.

So stand beneath their merry sway,
Catch a chuckle, come what may.
With giants who just love to jest,
In their laughter, we are blessed.

Echoes of the Whispering Woods

In a forest where humor grows,
Giggles echo, nobody knows.
A tree forgot where it had stood,
And danced around like it was good.

One tree said, "Hear my tall tale!"
While twirling leaves made quite a gale.
They shared laughs with every breeze,
Tickling trunks, they'd do as they please.

The bushes chimed in, "What a sight!
We're all here, let's take flight!"
As shadows pranced beneath the sun,
The woodlands laughed, it's all in fun.

So venture forth and hear their glee,
The echoes call from every tree.
With every shade and laughter shared,
The woods hold secrets, fun declared.

Whispers Between the Roots

Beneath the ground, the gossip flows,
Where squirrels plot and mischief grows.
A raccoon claims he's found the gold,
But it's just an acorn, or so I'm told.

The worms all giggle with glee and cheer,
As ants share laughs with a crooked sneer.
A dandelion joins, with a puff and a sigh,
'What's the fuss? It's just dirt and sky!'

The shadows dance, a playful tease,
While the roots hum tunes in the gentle breeze.
'Who's the tallest? Who's the best?'
The humble grass just laughs, no jest.

In the heart of the grove, a secret spills,
A tree once danced, oh what a thrill!
With branches swaying in wild delight,
The postcard must've been quite a sight!

The Lore of Lushness

Once in a grove lived a cheeky sprite,
Who sprinkled dew drops 'til the morning light.
The ferns all curled with a sassy flair,
While dandelions giggled without a care.

'Gather around, let the laughter run,'
Said the old oak, basking in sun.
With stories of cats who danced on moonbeams,
And rabbits who wore hats in their dreams.

The poplar winked, 'I can do a jig!'
While a willow bowed low, feeling quite big.
'But don't touch my leaves, they're way too fine!'
The breeze just chuckled, 'They're not divine!'

And so in the shade, chortles took flight,
Where roots knew the truth and hearts felt light.
The wisest stories are spun with glee,
For laughter's the root of the mighty tree!

Silhouettes in the Sundown

As the sun dipped low, the laughs grew loud,
While shadows stretched tall, forming a crowd.
The pine wore a hat made of flickering light,
Boasting of dreams that took off in flight.

With crickets composing a symphony sweet,
The raccoon pranced 'round on mischievous feet.
'Hey, have you heard what the fox has said?'
But the owls just hooted, 'We're all well-fed!'

The evening breeze wove a tapestry bright,
While dusk-soft whispers danced in the night.
'Who's got the best stories? Who's got the sound?'
They laughed and they spun, with joy all around.

Each silhouette pranced, a merry parade,
In hues of gold, the trees gently swayed.
So gather your tales, let the stories unwind,
In the dance of the dusk, true joy you'll find!

Echoing the Ages

In a grove where laughter echoes clear,
The stories of old are filled with cheer.
The mighty elder spoke with a grin,
'Have I told you how I learned to spin?'

With mischievous squirrels and chirping birds,
They flipped through the pages without words.
'Yesterday's gossip is today's fun,
Just listen close, under the sun!'

Each branch held a chuckle, each leaf a jeer,
While the roots chuckled, drinking cheer.
The wind whispered secrets, stirring the boughs,
'What do you say, shall we take a bow?'

So lift a glass to the wood and glade,
Where even the shadows have charades.
With echoes of ages, laughter ignites,
In the heart of the grove, where joy ignites!

Reveries in the Glimmering Grove

In a grove where the fireflies laugh,
The squirrels dance on a wooden giraffe.
They debate if acorns are better than cheese,
And giggle at owls with their snoozy wheeze.

A rabbit tells tales of a chicken that flies,
While butterflies peep, all aglow with surprise.
They tease the old roots that joke and complain,
Turning the rain into ticklish champagne.

Legends Beneath the Twisting Vines

Beneath the vines where the shadows twist,
A lizard once played the piano, I insist.
The frogs in the pond formed a loud, jolly band,
They croaked out their hits, hip-hop on land.

A deer with a top hat would smile and prance,
Saying, "Dance with me now! Take a chance!"
But the mushrooms just chuckled, wanting a seat,
In this vine-woven, whimsical retreat.

The Echoing Voice of the Oldest Oak

The oldest oak had a booming voice,
Telling fish stories, making squirrels rejoice.
"There once was a cat who thought he could swim,
He splashed in the brook, oh so grim!"

With each hearty laugh, a few branches shook,
Bouncing acorns like an open book.
The birds would snicker, losing their cool,
As stories grew taller, breaking every rule!

Milestones Marked in Moss

In a forest where landmarks are marked in green,
A worm claimed the title of being the queen.
She crowned herself with a leaf and said,
"I rule over puddles! Bow down to my spread!"

Nearby, the ants wove a carpet of crumbs,
While hedgehogs giggled, playing instruments of drums.
As the sun set low, the chatter grew loud,
And every last critter felt oh-so-proud.

The Poetics of Pine

In a grove full of pine, a squirrel took a stand,
With acorns as his props, he formed a funny band.
The trees all swayed, could barely hold their bark,
As the squirrel sang loudly from dawn until dark.

A chipmunk joined in, wearing a hat of leaves,
While branches whispered secrets, like gentle thieves.
With every silly line, the laughter would ignite,
And the forest echoed joy, from morning till night.

The Call of the Cedar

A cedar stood grand, with a wise, wobbly grin,
It chuckled at clouds when the rain would begin.
"Hey, fluffy white puffs, don't you fall down please!"
"I'm too soft for a shower; you'll mess up my trees!"

The wind roared with laughter, like a ticklish breeze,
Spinning stories around, among giggling leaves.
The birds joined the fun, mimicking every sound,
A concert of chaos, with laughs all around!

Timber Tales of Two Worlds

In a world up high, with birds dressed in style,
A beaver from below would visit for a while.
"Can you teach me to fly?" he asked with a grin,
The trees hooted loudly, "Let's see how you spin!"

With branches like arms, they guided his quest,
In odd little circles, he tried with his best.
He flopped and he flailed, splashing down like a splash,
While the owls hooted merry, and the whispers turned brash.

Conversations with Canopies

The canopies above, with gossip so sweet,
Chatting in whispers, like gossiping feet.
"Did you hear about Oak? He's sprouted a shoe,
A fashion so strange, it's the talk of the crew!"

Down below, the roots would giggle and sway,
As the ants marched in line, with a parade on display.
They'd tap-dance for fun, in a rhythmic delight,
While the trees burst in laughter, stretching left and right.

Parables of the Canopied Realm

In forest shade, the squirrels meet,
With acorn hats, they dance on feet.
The wise old owl just calls them fools,
While plotting pranks with all the ghouls.

A rabbit hops, his tail a blur,
He tells a joke that makes them stir.
The trees chuckle, their boughs a sway,
As laughter echoes through the day.

Murmurs from the Majestic Pines

The pines debate on who's the tallest,
A squirrel shouts, 'I'm the smallest!'
They argue 'til the night is late,
While shadows play a funny fate.

A woodpecker jokes about their height,
'You'll need a ladder to take flight!'
Their laughter rustles every leaf,
Nature's comedy beyond belief.

Ballads Beneath the Starlit Branches

Under twinkling lights, the critters sing,
A raccoon winks, 'I'll be the king!'
The fireflies flash a dance so bright,
As the trees sway, embracing the night.

An owl hoots, 'Who's ready for a show?'
The leaves respond with a breezy flow.
The stars all giggle at the rhyme,
In the woodlands' stage, there's no such time.

Narratives in the Grains of Wood

Each ring tells tales of laughter past,
Where tree folk gather in shadows cast.
A chipmunk claims he caught a breeze,
While dancing with the butterflies with ease.

A beaver joins, with tales of dams,
And how he tricks the villagers' clams.
With every story, the woods erupt,
In glee and giggles, forever corrupt.

The Great Green Story

In a forest thick with laughter,
The squirrels tell their jokes.
A dance upon the branches,
While sneaky raccoons poke.

The owls hoot in delight,
As foxes play tag below.
Each tree shakes with excitement,
As whispers to the moonflow.

Beneath the leafy canopy,
Mischief swirls like the breeze.
A woodpecker's knock, knock, knock,
Brings giggles from the trees.

So sit and hear their chatter,
With every rustle and sway.
The forest is a comedy,
With punchlines that won't fray.

Cryptic Conifers

Pine cones drop like secrets,
With whispers in the air.
A squirrel holds a meeting,
While shadows dance with flair.

The needles shine like laughter,
In the bright and dappled sun.
Mysteries of the forest,
Where every tree's a pun.

Spruce makes jokes about moss,
As fir laughs in the breeze.
They swap tall tales of weather,
With giggles through the leaves.

Elms join in the fun,
With jokes about their bark.
In this coniferous circus,
There's never a dull lark.

Dreams in the Dappled Light

In the quilt of sunlight,
Dreams weave through leafy seams.
A chipmunk spins a fancy,
While the day drifts in dreams.

A caterpillar wiggles,
With tales of munch and chew.
The butterflies are giggling,
As they play peekaboo.

The sunbeam's winking playfully,
As shadows dance around.
The trunks are laughing heartily,
In this merry, leafy ground.

Close your eyes and wander,
In this light of joy and cheer.
Each tickle of the branches,
Creates chuckles you can hear.

The Silence of Sturdy Branches

Sturdy branches hold their peace,
But whispers fill the air.
A rabbit stops to listen,
As if it's part of the flair.

The ants march in formation,
A parade of tiny glee.
While old oaks stand like statues,
With stories of the sea.

The breeze brings clever riddles,
As hardworking bees hum low.
"Who's the tallest in the forest?"
"Just look up, and you will know!"

Though silence seems prevailing,
Laughter lies just within reach.
The sturdy arms of nature,
Have a lot of joy to teach.

Lullabies of the Leafy Heights

In the branches high and merry,
Squirrels dance, their tales so cheery.
Raccoons gossip with a wink,
While the old owl gives a blink.

With a rustle, leaves drop low,
Tickling toes, 'Oh, what a show!'
Breezes laugh, the branches sway,
Nature's jests in bright display.

Underneath, the deer just sigh,
Wondering when they'll learn to fly.
But laughter echoes through the trees,
As chipmunks scamper with such ease.

In this playground up so high,
Every creature waves goodbye.
They'll return once the sun's down,
To share their joy across the town.

Stories Cradled by the Oak

Beneath the oak so big and round,
The best of pranks can be found.
With acorns falling, they play tricks,
Squirrels giggle, 'Look at this!'

A rabbit hops in quite a fuss,
Hastily seeking his lost bus.
The wise old crow caws with glee,
'Hop aboard, it's just a spree!'

Rabbits race, the sun dips low,
Beneath the leaves, they nimbly go.
Each twist and turn brings fresh delight,
Stories shared in the fading light.

The moon peeks through with a grin,
As the critters cackle, 'Let's begin!'
Each shadow tells a funny tale,
As laughter winds through every trail.

The Wisdom of the Whispering Glade

In the glade where whispers roam,
A frog claims it's the best of homes.
With every croak, a joke takes flight,
And bees buzz by, all day and night.

The flowers nod to each quip made,
While butterflies dance in the shade.
A tortoise slow, with a knowing smile,
Says, 'Patience pays off, just wait a while.'

A badger sneezes, stirs the frogs,
Who leap and laugh at passing dogs.
In this haven, silly and wise,
Laughter mingles with the skies.

With every breeze that comes and goes,
The glade shares wisdom only it knows.
In moments fleeting, joy is spun,
Till daylight fades, and dreams are fun.

Fables on a Forest Breeze

The wind whispers funny things,
Of dancing bears and feathered kings.
A porcupine gives fashion tips,
While frogs perform their funny flips.

Near bubbling brooks, the stories flow,
Fish leap out to steal the show.
With every splash and joyful song,
They tease the otters all day long.

Beneath the stars, a raccoon shouts,
'Who stole my snacks?' Amid the doubts.
Ghosts of trees laugh, spread the cheer,
As fireflies flicker bright and near.

The forest hums with silly plays,
Nighttime tales in a moonlit haze.
Each creature joins in the fun parade,
As fables dance in the sounds they made.

Legends Carved in Bark

Once a squirrel with quite a flair,
Danced on branches, without a care.
He claimed he could fly, oh what a sight,
But fell down laughing, his nuts in flight.

An owl hooted, wisdom to share,
"Do acorns taste better when you're in the air?"
The squirrel just winked, with a mischievous grin,
"In my next act, I'll juggle a pin!"

The raccoons joined, with masks on their face,
Said, "This little twirl is a grand showcase!"
But slipped on the leaves all yellow and brown,
They tumbled and giggled, lost in the gown.

So trees stood tall, with stories to crack,
Holding the laughter, never looking back.
For every slip and every fun jest,
Are etched in their rings, where dreams find rest.

Shadows of the Leafy Sentinels

In the cool shade, a lizard proclaimed,
"I'm the king here, forever unclaimed!"
But a bird above just cawed with a cheer,
"You're the king of bugs, my friend, I fear!"

The trees whispered softly, leaves all a-flutter,
While critters below laughed, some rolled in the gutter.
"Oh, mighty lizard, if you would just sing,
You'd reign over all, like the silliest king!"

The lizard perplexed, gave it a shot,
Bellowed a tune that was quite a lot.
But the song turned to hiccups, and giggles around,
As laughter erupted, spreading joy all around.

So shadows grew long, and stories got spun,
Of creatures both quirky, and always good fun.
For among the tall trunks, the laughter ran free,
Where every odd sight brought a glee-filled decree.

Chronicles Beneath the Sky High

Once a wise tree with branches so grand,
Met a gusty wind, that skipped on the land.
"Can you twirl like a dancer?" asked the tree, with glee,
"I'll show you some moves, just follow me!"

They spun in a whirl, as leaves took a flight,
The tree's boughs did tango, oh what a sight!
But the wind took a breath and with a loud puff,
Swirled the branches, and said, "This is tough!"

"Let's flip and let's flop, oh, what a great jest,
We'll invent a new dance, it'll be quite the fest!"
The critters all gathered, observing with glee,
As the trunk-dancing tree and the wind danced for free.

With laughter abounding, the sun started to glow,
The chronicles whispered, in breezy flow.
Each ripple of joy carved deep into bark,
Held secrets of laughter, like a sparkling spark.

Fables Woven by the Wind

A tiny mouse built a home in a nook,
Told tales of adventure, with every nook.
"I've traveled the fields, the hills and the bay,
Did you know I once outran a dog in play?"

The tree shook its branches, teasing a bit,
"Dear mouse, I've seen creatures with far greater wit!
You had better fortune than brains in that race,
But do tell me more, it will brighten this place!"

The mouse puffed with pride, in the sun's gleam,
"Last week, I scared off a hawk with my scream!"
But the tree chuckled deep, as the critters all heard,
"Wouldn't it be great if that hawk had just blurred?"

With whispers of wind, they spun yarns so fine,
Of mishaps and laughter, in loops like a vine.
For every small moment, every cheeky grin,
Lives in the stories, the breeze danced within.

Bark and Breeze: A Chronicle

In a forest where laughter flows,
Trees wear hats, and the wind just knows.
Squirrels hold dance-offs all day long,
Each acorn a beat, a silly song.

Breezes chuckle with the rustling leaves,
Sharing secrets that no one believes.
A parrot jokes, perched high on a bough,
His punchlines drop like rain, oh wow!

Bark peers in with a gnarled old grin,
"Who's that fool who can't find a pin?"
Roots twist and twirl beneath the ground,
In this merry kingdom, joy is found.

As shadows dance under the glowing moon,
The trees clap hands to the midnight tune.
Laughter echoes through the darkened glade,
Where stories of whimsy are always made.

Leaves that Listen

Up high where the chatter never stops,
Leaves lean in as the rumor drops.
"Did you hear the one about the old oak?
He lost his balance and gave a poke!"

Caterpillars giggle on a leafy throne,
Tickled by whispers from the trees they've grown.
The sunbeams wink through a tapestry bright,
While the breeze sneezes, "Oh what a sight!"

Branches wiggle like a dancing friend,
As owls wink back — they just pretend.
Underneath, roots are rolling in glee,
Shaking and cracking, "What will we see?"

Every leaf has a tale to share,
With chuckles and sighs hanging in the air.
In the canopy where giggles will bloom,
It's a riot of humor, a whimsical room.

Roots of Memory

Beneath the surface where secrets thrive,
Roots tell stories, keeping dreams alive.
"Remember when the wind tried to race?
It nearly tumbled us all, what a chase!"

The whispers weave through the earthy ground,
Each bend and twist a memory found.
Old fungi nod with a sponge-like grin,
"Our stories are gold, let the laughter begin!"

A mole pops up with a cheeky wink,
"Did you hear what the last tree did think?"
With chuckles resounding, they all convene,
Making mischief where no one's seen.

Every taproot has its own tune,
Making friends with the daisies in bloom.
In this world where roots dance and sigh,
Humor plants seeds that reach for the sky.

Chronicles in the Canopy

In the canopy where the stories drip,
Parrots gab, not one ever skips.
"Did you spot that sapling with flair?
He wears his leaves like a new hair!"

Branches twist in a theatrical play,
Giggling at shadows that scamper away.
Seas of green ripple with sweaty delight,
As sunbeams tickle the leaves, oh what a sight!

A beetle with glasses reads books on a bark,
While chipmunks propose a late night park.
In this woodland womb of chuckles and mirth,
Humor sprouts roots deep into the earth.

With each fleeting breeze, stories are spun,
In a chorus of laughter, the trees invite fun.
From thicket to trunk, the humor takes flight,
Under a canopy kissed by shimmering light.

A Symphony of Saplings

Little leaves laugh in the breeze,
Dancing to whispers of big old trees.
Squirrels twirl in acorn hats,
While birds jam with funky spats.

Buds peek out with cheeky grins,
Planning pranks on their sturdy kin.
Roots tickle toes of passing feet,
In this garden, mischief's a treat!

Tiny trunks boast of their height,
Claiming they'll outgrow the night.
Sunlight winks from above the crowd,
Shining bright and feeling proud.

Around the bark, a curious kid,
Listens to stories of what they did.
In every rustle and every creak,
Lies a joke from the tallest clique.

Chronicles of the Canopy

Branches gossip of the weather,
Chortling as they sway together.
Leaves are laughing, a merry crowd,
Joking that they're dressed too loud.

Swinging vines play tag with the sun,
While woodland critters laugh and run.
One cheeky owl named Fred,
Winks at the rabbit, "You're well-fed!"

A pine declares it's all a bluff,
"I'm the softest, and that's enough!"
But if you ask a wise old oak,
It'll tell you jokes that make you choke.

With every breeze, the fun takes flight,
Creating stories wrapped in delight.
So if you wander, take a look,
Join the laughter, oh, what a hook!

Beneath the Branches' Embrace

Shade provides a funny sight,
As squirrels play hide-and-seek with light.
Laughter echoes from the ground,
When a sleepy sloth tumbles down.

Leaves gossip, making chatter,
While ants debate on what's the matter.
"Why's the ground so far away?"
Cried out a young sprout in dismay.

The breeze carries whispers wide,
Of tall tales that will abide.
With roots that tickle and stretch so far,
The forest knows no dull memoir.

Under the arches, laughter flows,
As the moon starts to impose.
So take a seat and hear them cheer,
In this grove, joy's always near.

Giant Sentinels' Soliloquy

Oh, the secrets that they share,
Big trees bluff, and none can compare.
"I've weathered storms!" the oak declares,
While laughing softly at new affairs.

The cedar grins, "It's all a game,
Let's count the rings and stake our claim!"
Bark to bark, they share a jest,
Giant sentinels, never at rest.

In dappled light, shadows prance,
A frog jumps in, joins the dance.
"Do you think your height's a crown?"
They giggle, saying, "Look around!"

Trees may tower, but joy's the root,
Each twist and turn sparks a hoot.
Among their limbs, fun intertwines,
With laughter steeped in ancient vines.

The Songs of Strong Stems

In the forest, whispers play,
While squirrels dance and sway.
Branches twist, a goofy jig,
Echoing laughter with each big dig.

A woodpecker taps a silly tune,
As leaves bop under the moon.
They giggle whenever the wind blares,
Tickling trunks like gentle dares.

Sap drips down, a sweet delight,
A sticky trap for bugs at night.
The audience? Frogs in a choir,
Ribbeting along like they never tire.

So gather 'round for nature's tease,
Those sturdy stalks know how to please.
With every creak and quirky twist,
The woods become a comic tryst.

Skeins of Shadow and Sun

In patches of shadow, the laughter stirs,
As light filters down, the giggle occurs.
A sunbeam tickles a lazy hare,
He hops, then stops, with a startled stare.

The shadows play hide-and-seek, oh what fun!
A game involving everyone!
Owls blink at the antics of mice,
While the wind whispers secrets, oh so nice!

A mischievous squirrel steals a snack,
While a wise old tree gives him a smack.
With roots in the earth and branches up high,
They chuckle together, 'Oh my, oh my!'

Underneath this canopy's gleam,
Life swirls about like a wacky dream.
The shadows dance, and the sun gives chase,
In this joyful, wild, poetic space.

The Unfolding of Barkbound Histories

With each ring grown, a story's spun,
Of woodpeckers' pecks and rays of sun.
A gnarled old branch hums with glee,
'I'm the grandpa you all want to see!'

Amongst the roots, mischief brews,
As ants march by in tiny shoes.
They gossip about the great gusts of wind,
And how many acorns the blue jays pinned.

The bark grins wide with tales so bold,
Of worms that wriggle and mysteries told.
When raindrops fall, they slide and race,
Leaving behind a slippery space.

Laugh with the leaves, let spirits fly,
For nature's brief and silly reply.
In every crevice, humor's ripe,
A history written in giggles, a type!

Nature's Own Anthology

Gathered in green, an audience waits,
In the arms of beauty, laughter relates.
Bees buzz jokes from blossom to bud,
While frogs croak punchlines in the mud.

Each leaf a page, crisp and new,
Turning in breezes, sharing the view.
Stories flutter, oh what a sight,
As butterflies dance in sheer delight.

A pine stands tall, proclaiming its fame,
While berries blush, feeling quite lame.
The daisies giggle and dare to confess,
That even the thorns can get quite a mess.

So come, explore this quirky tome,
Where colors and chirps feel right at home.
In nature's book, joyous and bright,
The laughter echoes, day and night.

Carved in the Bark

Silly squirrels with nutty dreams,
Chase their tails in sunlit beams.
Whispers of laughter in the breeze,
As branches sway with joyous ease.

Old owls chuckle, wisdom's jest,
While woodpeckers drum at their best.
Leaves giggle softly, a rustling song,
Each barked laugh, where they belong.

Raccoon pranksters, masked with flair,
Sneak a snack from here to there.
In the shade, they plot and scheme,
Among the roots, they dance and dream.

Nature's jesters, life's delight,
In a world where mischief takes flight.
With every ring, a little cheer,
From rustling limbs, we'll always hear.

Moonlit Murmurs

Beneath the moon, secrets unfold,
With giggles of night critters bold.
Crickets serenade with song and flare,
While shadows twinkle without a care.

A wise old tree whispers tales so sly,
Of raccoons beneath the starry sky.
They trade their stories for a midnight snack,
As fireflies flicker, a glowing pack.

Bats swoop down with whispers of glee,
As shadows dance in playful esprit.
Laughter echoed in every crack,
As branches join in their merry attack.

In moonlit realms, where all's a jest,
Every rustle and twirl feels like a fest.
As nature pranks and plays all night,
The forest joins in with sheer delight.

The Wisdom of Evergreen

A grumpy pine stands tall and proud,
With needles sharp, not one a shroud.
He grumbles tales of windy foes,
Of acorns dropped and bending bows.

Ferns laugh quietly, swaying in jest,
"Dear sage of wood, you need a rest!"
Pine puffs up, then lets out a sigh,
"Just wait till spring, you'll see me fly!"

Every twig tells a joke or two,
As summer spills its vibrant hue.
Branches quiver with giggles amassed,
While whispers of laughter hold steadfast.

The wisdom wrapped in bark so bold,
Is woven with mirth; never grows old.
In every grain, a chuckle springs,
The laughter of nature eternally sings.

Stories Beneath the Stars

Under stars that twinkle bright,
The wind shares secrets of the night.
Mice tell tales in squeaks and scurries,
Of wild escapades and funny flurries.

Beetles waltz in a moonlit glow,
While fireflies put on quite a show.
Their little lights flick against the dark,
Sparking laughter in every park.

The grass leans in to catch each jest,
While crickets chirp, "We are the best!"
With every rustle, a giggle fades,
A symphony of nature's charades.

Beneath these stars, where stories grow,
Laughter ripples, glowing and low.
Each creature joins in the night's delight,
In a world where whimsy takes flight.

Sagas of the Sylvan Spirits

In the forest where the squirrels play,
The wise old owl has something to say.
He hoots and he laughs, a feathery bard,
Telling tales of a raccoon playing a card.

The rabbits jump high, doing flips in the air,
While deer spin around, their dance quite rare.
A fox sneaks in, wearing a hat,
Whispering secrets, "Did you see that cat?"

With mushrooms as bars and acorns as drinks,
The critters gather, exchanging their winks.
Each story they swap brings giggles and glee,
In a woodland where laughter is wild and free.

So when you wander through shrubs and trees,
Listen close, you'll hear the breeze.
It's filled with the chuckles from up above,
The spirit of fun in the woods they love.

The Arbor's Echo

Among the branches where shadows dart,
The giggles of squirrels play a big part.
They jest about acorns, the treasures they hoard,
And how they could be the next woodland lord.

A raccoon with a mask, so clever, so sly,
Dreams of his heists, under the moonlit sky.
But his plans are foiled by a bumbling old bear,
Who trips on a root, falling without a care.

The elder trees chuckle with hollowed-out glee,
At the antics of critters so reckless and free.
With roots intertwined, their stories entwined,
In the echoes of laughter, great joy we find.

And if you should wander through this lively glade,
Take heed of the fun from the shade that they've made.
For wisdom and humor in nature unite,
Creating a canvas of pure delight.

Whispers of the Woodlands

In the heart of the grove where the wildflowers play,
A crow caws a riddle, brightening the day.
With feathers a-shimmer and eyes full of cheer,
He finds it quite funny to jest with the deer.

Frogs on the pond throw a splashy big ball,
While turtles just chuckle, slow-moving but tall.
One says, "Why race? Let's blend in with the rush!"
And the hare replies, "You're right, that's a crush!"

The winds whisper jokes through the branches so high,
Each tree takes a turn, with a wink in its eye.
As the laughter rolls onward, from root to the crown,
Every creature joins in, dispelling the frown.

Beneath the green canopy, hearts intertwine,
With humor and mischief, it all feels divine.
So next time you stroll through the foliage bright,
Join in on the fun, let your spirit take flight.

Shadows in the Canopy

In shadows that dance where the sunlight gleams,
The trees share their whispers in fanciful themes.
With branches a-waving, they plot and they scheme,
A grove full of giggles, it's all like a dream.

A mischievous squirrel steals a hat from a frog,
The laughter erupts like a well-tempered fog.
They roll on the ground, oh, what a fine crew,
Making friends in the forest, all tied up in dew!

The branches rock gently, the leaves flutter wide,
As the fairies join in for a fun, joyful ride.
Swirling through petals in spirited bliss,
Each creature partakes in the merriment's kiss.

So venture on trails where the wild things roam,
And in the cool shade, you'll always feel home.
For amongst the tall giants, the laughter flows free,
Creating a comedy, nature's grand spree.

Starlit Stanzas of the Trees

Under the glow of a silver moon,
A squirrel wore a tiny balloon.
It danced with glee on a swaying limb,
While stars giggled softly, their light not dim.

A wise old owl in his cozy nook,
Shared tales of acorns and a funny book.
His glasses slipped, oh what a sight,
While raccoons cheered for the owl's delight.

The fireflies flickered, buzzing with cheer,
They lit the stage, bringing joy near.
A rabbit hopped in with a joke on tongue,
Causing the night to burst with fun.

At dawn, the trees shared a laugh so loud,
Of squirrels juggling nuts, oh what a crowd!
With twinkling leaves in a merry spree,
They whispered and chuckled, wild and free.

Wind-Swept Chronicles

The breeze told secrets with a playful twist,
As leaves whirled round like they couldn't resist.
A chipmunk chimed in, perched high and proud,
Claiming he'd dance to a song from the cloud.

Old pines cracked jokes about shoes made of bark,
While the maples humored them with a spark.
Each gusty gust brought laughter alive,
As willows swayed in a comedy drive.

With acorns tumbling, a playful brigade,
The trees hosted games in the sun and the shade.
A raccoon's mischief sent giggles around,
As laughter bounced high, unconfined and unbound.

The wind joined in, a merry sound wave,
Telling tall tales of how trees misbehave.
In whispering laughter, all came to agree,
Nature's a jester, as funny as can be.

The Language of Leaves

Leaves chattered softly in a vibrant green,
Exchanging gossip on the funny scene.
A parrot swooped in, feathers aflutter,
Said, "You won't believe, a snail danced a strut!"

The birch cracked wise about weathered old trunks,
While oaks guffawed, sporting their flunks.
Breezes tickled branches, laughter took flight,
As pine needles shivered in sheer delight.

A clever woodpecker chimed with a beat,
Claiming each tap was a funny tweet.
They all sang together, a raucous refrain,
As the sun began to smile over the plain.

In rustling joy, the language was clear,
With every chuckle, the world would draw near.
Nature's own humor, alive in the air,
Each leaf knew a joke, a story to share.

Beneath the Arbor's Embrace

Beneath the branches, a gathering formed,
With critters and creatures, vibrant and warmed.
A fox told a tale of a shoe left behind,
While laughter erupted, a secret so blind.

The rabbits brought snacks, all fluffy and bright,
With cucumbers dancing, a joyous sight.
They feasted on puns about carrots in hats,
While squirrels debated the size of their chats.

The elder trees chuckled at squirrels' delight,
Whispering wisdom, both silly and bright.
As shadows grew longer, and night crept in,
They promised more fun when the day would begin.

In the heart of the wood, where the giggles ignite,
Magic in laughter twinkled at night.
With roots deep in humor, they swayed and they spun,
In a circle of joy, where all is just fun.

Sagas of the Silver Spruce

In the forest where shadows play,
A spruce claimed, 'I had quite a day!'
Raccoons came to dance, oh what a sight,
The owl hooted, 'You guys are light!'

Squirrels leaped, all full of glee,
Chasing each other up to the tree.
'You can't catch me!' the youngest would shout,
While the grumpy old crow just flapped about.

Acorns fell like tiny bombs,
As laughter echoed, oh, how it calms.
A chipmunk declared, 'I'm the best at hide!'
And promptly tripped, with laughter the prize.

Under the stars, they'd sit and spin,
The wild, tall tales they'd claim as wins.
Each night brought joy, each dawn delight,
In the grove, fun reigned both day and night.

Age-Old Whispers

The oak grinned wide, his bark all cracked,
He said, 'I've seen a raccoon who snacked!'
With berries and nuts, he thought it was gold,
But what a prank—now that's rich and bold!

Birch trees giggled, their leaves all aflutter,
'Oh, remember that time with the sneaky mutter?'
Where foxes met owls and offered a trade,
'Just don't say a word, or I'll get betrayed!'

Pinecones rolled in the breezy air,
The trees spun tales with mischievous flair.
While laughter rumbled through roots and leaves,
Nature's delight, as everyone believes.

In the twilight glow, they chatter and cheer,
Whispers of mischief, all filled with beer.
Round and round, the stories would share,
With every tall trunk giving a glare!

Reflections on Ridges

On the ridge, where winds love to tease,
A tree made a face—says, 'Look at these bees!'
Buzzing and fussing in silly retreat,
Thinking they're scary, oh what a feat!

The willows danced with the playful breeze,
Telling the birch to drop down her leaves.
'Let's make a wig!' the old willow cried,
While poor birch chuckled and shook with pride.

The view held secrets, the roots had grace,
Each twist and turn, a comical race.
'Who says trees can't groove, can't sway?'
With laughter echoing, night turned to day.

As the sun set low, they all took a bow,
With branches raised high, they shared a wow.
A ridge full of giggles, a night well spent,
In the company of friends, all laughter-sent.

Foliage Fairytales

Among the leaves, where flushes parade,
A tall tale of gnomes with hats that weighed.
They wobbled and giggled, tripped over roots,
And lost their way in bright dancing boots!

With acorns as marbles, they schemed with delight,
Said one little sprite, 'Let's race through the night!'
Zooming and zipping, what a fine jest,
But the moonbeams snickered and gave them a test.

'The highest of folly is surely a treat,'
Said the elder fern, with nimble little feet.
'Twist and twirl, oh don't you dare stop,
For the best of the fun is the flip and the flop!'

Under the stars, their laughter would rise,
Foliage fairytales beneath velvet skies.
With wild little wishes, they brightened the gloom,
Turning the forest into their amusing room.

Secrets in the Sap

A squirrel found a hat, so grand,
He wore it proudly, wasn't it planned?
He danced with glee, a funny sight,
As branches shook in pure delight.

A wise old owl with specs so round,
Said, "Keep your secrets from the ground!"
The tree trunk chuckled, roots would grin,
As whispers echoed from within.

The saplings giggled, a prank to play,
By sticking leaves in the sun's bright ray.
The sunbeams laughed and took a peek,
"What silly games these young do seek!"

A pinecone fell, went thud on a shoe,
"Catch me if you can!" it said, "I'm new!"
The trees all shook with laughter deep,
While ants marched by, they'd not lose sleep.

The Spirit of the Seasons

The winter's breeze brought laughter near,
With snowflake pranks that brought good cheer.
The branches danced to a frosty tune,
While snowmen winked 'neath the full moon.

In springtime bloom, a bee wore shades,
It buzzed around, played silly charades.
Blossoms chuckled as petals flew,
"Oh, look at that! Just one more view!"

Summer's sun pretended to hide,
Behind a cloud, where squirrels abide.
They played hide and seek with the rays,
And laughed aloud for countless days.

Once autumn came, leaves spun in glee,
As laughter echoed from tree to tree.
They formed a circle, shared a toast,
To the funny spirits they loved the most.

Echoes of the Evergreen

An evergreen chuckled, a funny joke,
To a passing bird, it quietly spoke.
"Why do trees love fancy clothes?
Because we all need to impress our shows!"

The bird just chirped and flapped with flair,
As pine needles ruffled in the air.
"You won't believe the stories I hear,
The woods are wild, buzzing with cheer!"

A raccoon danced in the moonlit grove,
With acorns bouncing, the trees did strove.
"Hey, don't drop that!" shouted old Birch,
"Or you'll summon a squirrel for a perch!"

Echoes of laughter rang through the leaves,
Under the canopies, where no one grieves.
Nature's humor, wild and free,
Lifts the spirits of you and me.

Riddles in the Rainforest

A sloth told riddles, slow as molasses,
"Why did the monkey wear funky glasses?"
The vines entwined, in giggles they shook,
While toucans chuckled in every nook.

The frogs croaked tunes as a dance ensued,
Splashing in puddles, feeling so good.
"Jump like us, it's all in the fun!"
As rain dripped down, they leaped and spun!

Laughter erupted when a parrot would tease,
"I flew around to find the best breeze!"
But tripped on a branch, it fell in a mess,
The rainforest roared, it couldn't do less!

With every drop, a story was spun,
In the heart of the jungle, where joy's never done.
The trees stood tall with a sense of pride,
While chuckles echoed far and wide.

Nature's Ancient Echo

In the grove where brambles twist,
Squirrels chat like gossiping mist.
A wise old oak with leaves so green,
Claims he's seen what's never been.

When the wind starts to laugh and giggle,
It tickles the bark, oh what a wiggle!
With every rustle, a secret shared,
The trees know things that leave us scared!

From crows who plot wicked plans at night,
To raccoons that dance in the moonlight.
Nature's stories, a quirky spree,
Whispered through branches, come climb a tree!

So raise a toast to the woods so wide,
Where humor and mystery like to hide.
Join the fun, don't miss your chance,
For a giggle in nature is the best romance!

Forest Folktales

In the heart of a forest, laughter roars,
Where trees tell jokes as they open their doors.
A pine spins yarns of encountering bears,
While willows sway, as if pulling hairs!

A deer with a crown thinks he's a king,
And the rabbits giggle at the songs he sings.
As the owls hoot in their scholarly glee,
The bushes chuckle, 'Who needs TV?'

Mice run marathons under the stars,
While beetles debate their shiny cars.
The forest floor's a stage to play,
Where every critter steals the show each day!

When the sun sets low and the shadows blend,
These lively tales seem to never end.
So listen closely, take a hike,
For in every rustle, a story's hike!

The Scrolls of Verdant Grace

Beneath a leafy umbrella, secrets scheme,
Each twig a pen, in nature's dream.
Birch trees whisper, "Did you hear?"
"Fred the frog just lost his beer!"

The hedgehogs chuckle, rolling in grass,
While chatty crows argue who's the sass.
With every breeze, the gossip flows,
And every tree, just likes to pose!

A turtle with shades claims he's so cool,
While ants invade, forming their school.
"Where's the class?" yells a bug on a leaf,
"Right here, buddy! Let's be brief!"

When night heralds with crickets' sound,
The forest joins in with dance profound.
So come one, come all, to relish this place,
Where laughter lingers in verdant grace!

Harmony in the Helix

Twisting branches reach for the skies,
While the pinecones gossip and share their lies.
A twisty vine starts to prance,
Inviting all to join the dance!

Frogs croak jokes that leave us in stitches,
While the dragonflies flaunt their glitches.
Where ferns flutter and pine trees snicker,
Laughter echoes, ever quicker!

Each rustling leaf has a tale to tell,
Of squirrels and acorns, and who raised hell.
So come spin a yarn with the foliage crew,
And find the fun in the green and blue!

Harmony rests where the laughter lives,
In the trees where each critter gives.
So join the ruckus, let your spirit flare,
As nature sings its song without a care!

When the Wind Speaks

Leaves giggle high as they sway,
Whispers of joy in a breezy play.
Branches bounce with a playful tease,
Rustling laughter dances with ease.

Squirrels scamper, their tails in a twirl,
Chasing each other in a dizzy whirl.
The wind tells stories, a raucous delight,
While birds perform acrobatics in flight.

Old oaks chuckle at every joke,
As shadows of laughter begin to cloak.
Underneath, roots wiggle with glee,
Please, oh please, let the fun never flee!

And when night falls, with a hoot and a caw,
The trees shake hands with a friendly paw.
In the moonlight, they wink and weave,
A comedy show, if you just believe.

The Verdant Gossamer

Beneath tangled vines, the smiles grow,
Witty butterflies put on a show.
Daisies giggle in gleeful rows,
As secrets of springtime quietly flows.

A slow-witted snail thinks he's a knight,
Daring the beetle to join in the fight.
But laughter erupts, and the joke's on him,
As he slips on a leaf, his chances seem slim.

The sunlight dances with prancing beams,
Tickling the petals, igniting their dreams.
Mossy carpets invite a quick rest,
In this space where humor feels blessed.

At twilight, the magic takes on a tune,
Fireflies twinkle; the night feels like noon.
Each gossamer thread, a tale of its own,
In this vibrant garden, roars of laughter are sown.

Guardians of Time

Beneath the watchful branches, a story unfolds,
Of wise old trees with bark like folds.
Their bark is full of laughter and cheer,
While critters dance, flapping with fear.

The knotty gnome gives a cheeky grin,
Spinning yarns in a big tree win.
With every turn of the steadfast ring,
Old leaves laugh at the silliness they bring.

Time ticks slow where shadows play,
As acorns gather to gossip all day.
A wooden squirrel shares a pun or two,
Knows that laughter is evergreen too.

When the sun sets, humor takes flight,
As fireflies buzz in the fading light.
Ancient guardians, with laughter divine,
Hold secrets of joy in the passage of time.

Fables in the Foliage

In wind-kissed glades, a tale takes root,
Of cheeky critters in a woodland suit.
A raccoon dons a hat, oh so fine,
While a wise owl keeps watch, sipping brine.

The bushes chirp, a chorus of giggles,
As frogs play leapfrog and dance in squiggles.
With every rustle and shiver of leaves,
Nature bursts forth; this mischief deceives.

Amidst the branches, a laughter-filled prison,
Where even the winds hum a funny vision.
The soft sighs of trees share humor so grand,
While squirrels concoct tricks just for the band.

Even the sun, behind clouds it peeks,
Chuckling softly, as mirthfully it sneaks.
Fables written in the whispers of green,
Have all the woodland chuckling, unseen.

The Weave of Wilderness

In the forest's tangled mess,
A raccoon wears a fancy dress.
It twirls beneath the moonlit sky,
While squirrels cheer and jump nearby.

A woodpecker drums a silly beat,
As hummingbirds dance on tiny feet.
The owl hoots jokes, and what a sight,
As critters gather for the night.

The trees gossip in leafy tones,
About antics of wild, feathered clones.
They chuckle at the antics bold,
Of little ones who dare be told.

So listen well to nature's cheer,
For laughter's near when trees are here.
With every breeze and rustling leaf,
There's humor wrapped in nature's brief.

Stories in the Sapwood

A chipmunk claims he found a hat,
Declares himself a royal brat.
He struts about, so proud and vain,
While all the birds just laugh and feign.

In the canopy, a parrot sings,
Of secret quests that nature brings.
It tells of nuts and acorn woes,
And how the wind played with their clothes.

The trees nod along with creaky sound,
As whispers echo through the ground.
A game of tag with shadows grand,
While sunbeams race and play on sand.

So if you roam beneath their shade,
Remember fun in nature made.
For every branch and every root,
Holds silly secrets in pursuit.

The Unseen Chronicles of the Grove

In the grove where shadows dance,
A badger dreams of romanced chance.
He wears a crown made of soft grass,
And claims to be the king, alas!

The rabbits hold a hop-along,
They giggle at the strangest song.
Singing loudly, hopping high,
While the wise old fox rolls by.

A spindly tree with branches bent,
Whispers woes of time well spent.
Squirrels plot and chatter low,
While acorns drop—a comical show.

So stroll along where laughter weaves,
Among the bark and all the leaves.
For in this place of jokes and cheer,
Nature's funny side is always near.

The Pulse of the Park

In the park where the bushes gossip low,
A turtle claims he's the fastest, though.
He races snails and boasts aloud,
While flowers bloom and nod so proud.

The ducks wear shades; they take their dive,
Pretending they're the hippest alive.
While turtles laugh, and squirrels view,
This park is a stage for nature's crew.

A wind-up toy, the grasshoppers spring,
Creating chaos, a buzzing fling.
While trees sway and giggle in time,
With every bark, a punchline rhyme.

So come and join this merry scene,
Where critters joke and never mean.
For in the pulse of leafy art,
Laughter thrives with every heart.

Legends Beneath the Leaves

In a whispering breeze, the squirrels conspire,
With acorn hats on, they build a high fire.
Telling tall tales of a cat that wore shoes,
And danced through the forest like it had the best moves.

The owls roll their eyes, saying, 'That's such a lie!'
But giggles escape from a passing fly.
"Just wait until dawn, we'll see who's the champ!"
As the trees swayed and the shadows did stamp.

Twigs became swords, as the rabbits all fought,
With epic adventures, each battle was sought.
"Did you hear the one about the fox in disguise?"
As laughter erupted and leaves took to skies.

Beneath rustling boughs where the mischief does brew,
Nature's own jesters write stories anew.
With the chirping of crickets, the night in a spin,
Legends abound where the wild things begin.

Echoes of the Ancient Grove

In the depths of the woods, the trees start to giggle,
Mushrooms are dancing; the shadows all wiggle.
A deer in a tutu pranced through the glade,
While bees wore tiny hats, delighted and swayed.

The frogs croaked a chorus in silly old rhymes,
While fireflies flickered, keeping pace with the chimes.
'Oh, have you heard of the gopher who sings?'
He serenades the night with a tune fit for kings!

Branches doubled over with laughter so light,
As chattering birds shared a story at night.
Whispering mosses joined in on the fun,
Creating a symphony, the night had begun.

As echoes reverberate through shadows and leaves,
The woods hold their secrets, but laughter deceives.
For in the ancient grove where the stories take flight,
A humorous truth wraps the silence of night.

Forest Secrets Unveiled

What secrets lie hidden beneath leafy crowns?
A raccoon named Larry wore mismatched brown gowns.
He claimed to have seen, in a great flash of skill,
A turtle on roller skates, footloose and ill.

The rabbits all giggled and shook with delight,
'That's the fastest old turtle we've seen take a flight!'
They gathered 'round trees for a forest-wide show,
As Larry recounted the most ludicrous blow.

The wise old owl hooted, "Let's gather for tea!"
To hear more grand tales of the nightly spree.
But no one could focus; they chuckled and sighed,
At Larry's great stories, with laughter as guide.

So in woods full of wonders, the secrets unfold,
With humor and mischief as the fabric they hold.
For in every soft rustle and whimsical sound,
Are giggles and glee in the flora around.

The Storytellers of the Forest

Beneath boughs of wisdom, the storytellers meet,
Where critters abound, and laughter's a treat.
A tortoise recites from a pebbly old tome,
While chipmunks provide an animated home.

The hedgehogs all desire a spot by the fire,
To listen as tales climb ever higher.
'Once there was a bear who couldn't quite dance,'
And wooed all the bees with an awkward advance.

The foxes roll dice made of shiny pine nuts,
Rigging new games with playful big cuts.
They beam with delight, from thy branches above,
Creating a world made of friendship and love.

But every good story needs laughter and cheer,
As laughter echoes and twirls through the year.
So climb up your branches, let go of the stress,
Join the chorus of joy—our forest's success!

Life Lines of the Land

In the forest where the branches sway,
A squirrel debated on what to say.
He sniffed at the wind, thought it was a treat,
But it turned out to be a lost dog's feet.

The owls were laughing, they hooted with glee,
As the hedgehog danced in a wild jamboree.
They twirled 'round the roots, under the glow,
While rabbits clopped hooves, putting on a show.

The trees, they chuckled, their bark full of cheer,
As the ants formed a line, all marching in gear.
They carried a crumb, it was quite the delight,
For a feast in the shade, the party tonight!

When the sun set low, the laughter took flight,
With cicadas all buzzing, a magical night.
In life's little moments, the woods found their bliss,
As nature's own jesters, they laughed in the mist.

Murmurs of Moss and Mist

Moss on the rocks whispered secrets of old,
While the breeze teased ferns, daring them to be bold.
A snail in a hurry slipped right on a leaf,
And the frogs in the pond met his plight with disbelief.

The mist twirled around like a playful young sprite,
Tickling the branches, it danced in the light.
A crow cawed a joke, but no one took blame,
When the fish told the trees they all looked the same.

Mushrooms just giggled, so happy and spry,
As raccoons played peek-a-boo, always awry.
The wise old oak chuckled, "What's life without jest?"
While the critters all chirped, feeling truly blessed.

In a world full of whimsy, the laughter won't cease,
With each silly moment, the forest finds peace.
For in every nook, every cranny we see,
Lies the joy of the wild, oh, how fun it can be!

Shadows and Stories

In the shade of the birch, a shadow took flight,
With a pair of old socks giving quite the fright.
A rabbit in stripes, looking dapper and neat,
Planned a soirée for all, with a toast to the beet.

The fox, feeling suave, wore a hat made of pine,
While the turtles debated on who had the shine.
The winds whispered jokes, they'd tickled the leaves,
With each rustling laugh, the forest relieves.

There were whispers of romance between willows that swayed,
As the sun set the scene, it was nature's parade.
The fireflies flickered, like stars in a fable,
Bringing magic to life, as they danced 'round the table.

So gather the critters, let's share a good cheer,
For the shadows embrace all that's funny and dear.
With each twist and turn of the evening's weak light,
The woods spun a yarn to enchant through the night.

Silenced Roots

In a patch of soft earth where the roots like to lounge,
Lived a family of moles, with a sly little scrounge.
They giggled and whispered, their secrets quite deep,
While the grumpy old turtle just wanted to sleep.

A beetle with swagger rolled past in a flair,
Claiming his treasure, a shiny old chair.
The others all snickered, they just couldn't cope,
At the sight of a bug trying hard to elope.

The grasshoppers leapt with glee in their song,
While the crickets debated who really was wrong.
A breeze through the branches spread tales of delight,
As the roots intertwined, trading gossip by night.

Through the laughter and joy, the misunderstood flow,
The echoes of nature remind us to glow.
For life in this kingdom is funny, it seems,
With every ruckus fulfilling our dreams.

The Arbor's Ancient Memory

In the breeze whispers a story,
How squirrels dance in all their glory.
With acorns flying, oh what a sight,
The branches laugh with sheer delight.

A raccoon's heist, a clumsy blunder,
Makes all the branches shake like thunder.
They giggle soft, in rustling glee,
As the forest holds its breath in spree.

A woodpecker got the best of a joke,
While the owls hoot, 'What a bloke!'
Under leaves, the secrets play,
In the sun-dappled, lighthearted fray.

Secrets in the Shade

Under leafy canopies, shadows prance,
A mouse once tried to lead a dance.
With tiny feet and a big dream,
He tripped and tumbled—what a scream!

Old wise owls, perched with a grin,
Chuckle at antics that make them spin.
A frog's serenade, a croaky cheer,
Echoes through the leaves so near.

The breeze carries chuckles far and wide,
As bugs line up for the fun to bide.
In the shade, they're plotting anew,
With every leaf, the laughter grew.

The Forest's Heartbeat

In the hush, a tickle-do,
The trees' humor, who knew?
With every sway, their laughter flows,
A secret joy, as nature glows.

The woodlands hum with witty bites,
Chasing shadows and daring flights.
A chipmunk champions a racquetball,
A game where tiny creatures sprawl.

Caterpillars plotting mischief sweet,
As mushrooms giggle 'neath their feet.
Nature sings with every beat,
A symphony in green, so neat.

Tales of the Verdant Towers

Amongst the boughs, stories sprout,
Of creatures bold and moments stout.
A deer that twirled to a froggy tune,
Under the watch of a silly raccoon.

Mushrooms in a circle, a dance to ignite,
As fireflies join in the soft twilight.
The branches lean in, secrets to share,
Of mischief and glee in the cool evening air.

Beneath the stars, the forest plays,
With laughter echoing through the ways.
An endless joke for all to see,
In this grand, green comedy.

Nature's Narrative

In the shade, the squirrels jest,
With acorns flying, they're the best.
Barking dogs join in the cheer,
While wise old owls sip a beer.

The chipmunks dance, their tiny feet,
Tap-tap-tapping to a beat.
A raccoon with a hat so fine,
Sings ballads with a glass of wine.

Frogs croak loudly, out of tune,
While insects buzz a silly croon.
The rabbits giggle, tails in tow,
As flowers bloom in a bright show.

Clouds above, they laugh and race,
The sun plays peek-a-boo, a face.
In this realm of green delight,
Joy is found in every sight.

Canopy Conversations

Leaves whisper secrets, soft and sweet,
While branches woven dance to the beat.
A chatty bluebird, perched so high,
Comments on clouds as they float by.

The bees conspire in buzzing tones,
Plotting out their sweet honey loans.
A mischievous raccoon, quick and sly,
Tries to swipe a snack, oh my!

Dancing shadows play on the ground,
While footloose deer leap all around.
With every creak, the tall trees sway,
As if to say, "Let's laugh today!"

The wind joins in with a playful rush,
Tickling leaves in a gentle hush.
Nature's chat is a joyful spree,
What a delightful symphony!

Reverberations of the Wild

Bears breakdance in the moonshine glow,
As crickets play a banjo show.
Porcupines giggle at silly jokes,
While owls wink at the midnight folks.

Frogs in bow ties sing out loud,
While the trees nod, mighty and proud.
A fox in shades strolls with flair,
Claiming he's the forest's heir.

With every rustle, laughter trails,
The wind carries their clever tales.
All creatures gather for the fun,
Under the watch of the big, bright sun.

The river chuckles as it flows,
Tickling rocks that wear mossy clothes.
The forest's voice, both rich and wild,
Echoes laughter, carefree and wild.

Fables of the Forest Floor

Bugs on chairs sip morning dew,
While earthworms share tales, ancient and true.
A ladybug dresses to impress,
With tiny polka dots, oh, what a mess!

The mushrooms giggle, wise and round,
As playful raccoons scurry around.
Grasshoppers leap in a dance of cheer,
Celebrating nature, far and near.

A wise old tortoise joins the scene,
With stories that are quite routine.
Yet every tale brings a new delight,
Laughter echoes through day and night.

When shadows stretch, the laughter roars,
And even the roots have cracking scores.
In this realm of jest and glee,
The forest whispers, "Come play with me!"

Whispers of the Woodland Canopy

In the branches where squirrels conspire,
Acorns drop and cause a quagmire.
A chattering clan of birds so bright,
Debate on who's the best at flight.

A raccoon in a mask steals a snack,
While wise old owls just laugh at the pack.
Badgers gossip about the moon's shiny face,
While everyone hides in their leafy space.

The pine trees sway with a giggle so grand,
Tickling the clouds with a playful hand.
Each trunk a storyteller in disguise,
Holding secrets known only to the skies.

When the sun sets low and shadows grow long,
The forest hums out a whimsical song.
At the heart of it all, such jests come alive,
In the canopy's laughter, we joyfully thrive.

Stories Beneath the Ancient Boughs

Beneath the branches where stories entwine,
A hedgehog rolls up, just to dine.
The rabbits gather for a comedy night,
Cracking jokes till they're out of sight.

A deer shares tales of a dance gone wrong,
Paws slipping and sliding in a merry throng.
The ancient bark rolls its eyes with glee,
As wily foxes plot tricks by the tree.

With a rustle of leaves, the laughter takes flight,
As creatures convene in the warm twilight.
Sharing mishaps from the day's adventures,
Each laugh a note in the joy's greatest ventures.

The moonlight beams on the woodland's embrace,
Lighting the smiles on each furry face.
A chorus of snickers fills the sweet air,
In the heart of the forest, no worries to wear.

Echoes of the Forest Elders

Underneath the old oak's vast shade,
Whispers of wisdom and laughter parade.
The chipmunks gather to hear the wise,
As the squirrel's antics leave all in surprise.

Each wrinkle on bark tells a twisty jest,
Of wild antics that nature suggests.
Who knew a raccoon could dance like a pro?
While the wise old crow caws, 'Steal the show!'

A bonfire night with a flickering glow,
The stories get taller with every elbow.
Fables get launched by the light of the moon,
While fireflies flicker to the beat of the tune.

In the shadows where echoes take flight,
The laughter of critters dances in the night.
A festival of joy, of whimsy and mirth,
Where the heart of the forest finds its true worth.

Secrets of the Sapling Serenade

In a glen where the young trees sway with cheer,
Saplings giggle as the critters draw near.
Their branches too short for grand tales to spread,
They share little secrets from dawn until dread.

A mischievous breeze whispers in their ear,
"Gossip of sunshine, come gather near!"
With leaves fluttering like hands in delight,
Each sapling claps as they plan for the night.

A toad croaks a rhyme from the bottom of a pit,
While brambles chuckle, not willing to quit.
The shadows erupt into bursts of pure glee,
As the forest floor jiggles with life's jubilee.

Under the stars, the young saplings admire,
The tall trees above who inspire their fire.
With laughter resounding, the woods play along,
In the sweetness of nature, we all sing our song.

www.ingramcontent.com/pod-product-compliance
Lightning Source LLC
Chambersburg PA
CBHW051657160426
43209CB00004B/934